**SCHOLASTIC**

# NAVIGATING NONFICTION

## by Alice Boynton and Wiley Blevins

Credits appear on page 96 which constitutes an extension of this copyright page.

ISBN-13 978-0-439-78302-6
ISBN-10 0-439-78302-X

# Table of Contents

# Amazing Nests!

Birds find different things in nature to make their nests.

hummingbird

oriole

## Plants, Spit, Webs

A hummingbird makes a nest with plants. It uses its sticky spit to hold the plants together. Spit isn't the only sticky stuff in the nest. The bird uses spiderwebs to stick the nest to a **pinecone**.

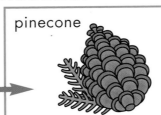

pinecone

## Soft Grass

An oriole makes a nest with grass. It weaves soft grass together with other things. The long nest hangs from a **branch**. Enemies can't get the eggs inside the nest.

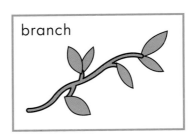

branch

# What Do You See?

Put a ✓ next to the features you see in <u>Amazing Nests</u>!

| | |
|---|---|
| [✓] | **1** title |
| [✓] | **2** introduction |
| [✓] | **3** photos |
| [✓] | **4** labels |
| [✓] | **5** special print<br>**bold** words    color print    large print    <u>underlined</u> words |
| [ ] | **6** characters |
| [✓] | **7** special drawings    diagram    map |
| [✓] | **8** sub headings |

Bear Facts

**Black Bears**
Black bears live in forests and swamps in North America.

**Polar Bears**
Polar bears live in icy regions around the North Pole.

# How Are Teddy Bears Made?

The teddy bear is one of America's favorite toys. Here's how a teddy bear is made.

### ❶ Sketch It

An artist draws a picture of a bear. Then she makes a pattern. That is a plan to show what the bear will look like.

### ❷ Cut It Out

This worker lays a machine on fuzzy fabric. The machine cuts out many bear parts. It is like a cookie cutter.

### ❸ Sew It Up

All of the bear parts are sewn together by machine. Then the parts are ready to be filled with stuffing.

# Show What You Know!

Reread <u>From Apples to Applesauce</u>. Then, fill in the chart below. Draw a picture for each step.

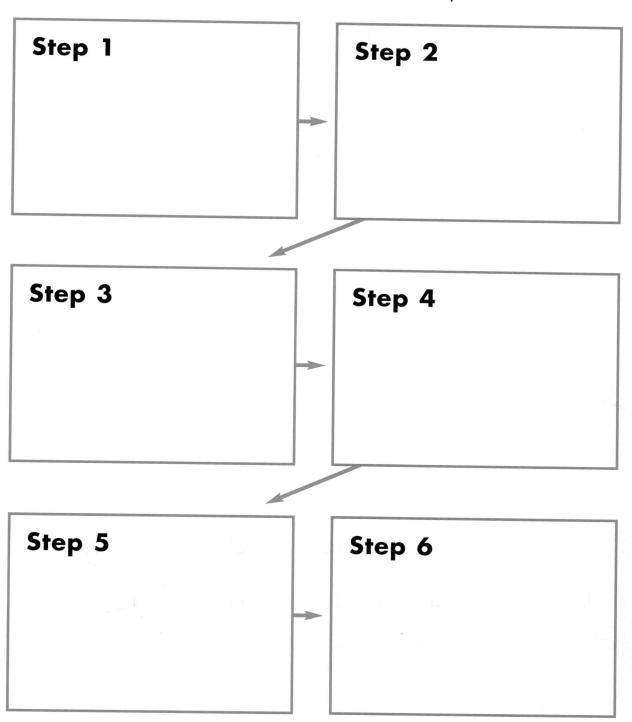

**Step 1**

**Step 2**

**Step 3**

**Step 4**

**Step 5**

**Step 6**

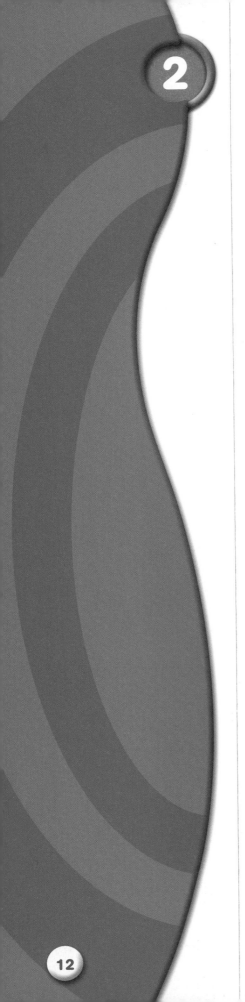

# The Amazing Emperor Penguin

## An Amazing Bird

It's hard to imagine anything living in Antarctica. But something does—the **emperor penguin**. Emperor penguins are large birds, but they don't fly. They are excellent divers and swimmers, however.

In March, winter comes to Antarctica. It is in winter that the mother emperor penguin lays one egg. Then she leaves! She goes into the icy waters to feed.

## Caring for the Egg

What happens to the egg? The father emperor penguin takes care of it. He balances the egg on the top of his feet. He keeps the egg warm and cozy by covering it with his pouch.

Each father stands with an egg on his feet for two months, through ice-cold days and nights, freezing winds, and **blizzards**. When does he eat? He doesn't! Not for two whole months.

To keep warm, all the fathers do an amazing thing. They huddle together tightly and take turns shuffling into the center. It's warmer there, because it's out of the cold wind. All this is done with an egg on their feet!

## A Chick Is Born

In May, the baby penguins, called **chicks**, hatch. Soon after, the mother penguins come back from the sea bringing food for their chicks. Then the hungry fathers can finally go to sea to feed.

## A Cold, Cold Place

Way, way down at the very bottom of the earth, there's a very big island. It's covered with ice and snow all year round. It's called **Antarctica**. Antarctica is the coldest place on Earth!

North America

Africa

South America

**Antarctica**

13

## Retell

Cut out the pictures. Use them to retell <u>The Amazing Emperor Penguin</u>.

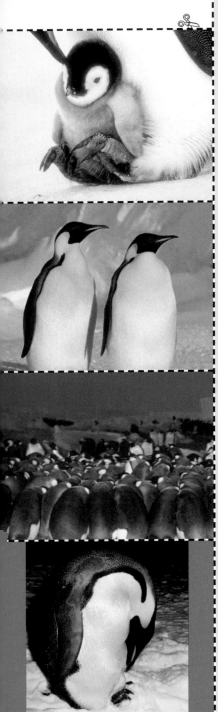

# Learning Log

The pictures are all mixed up! Put them in the right order. Number them 1, 2, 3.

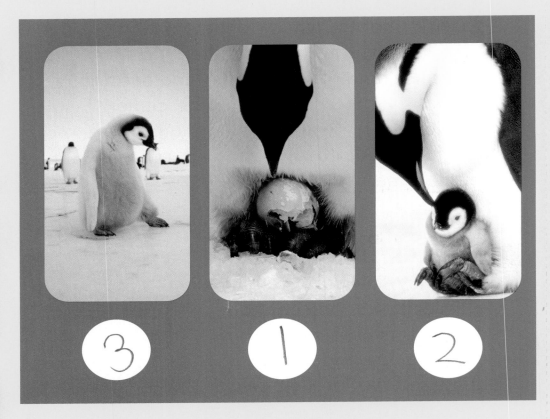

3   1   2

 **What happens after the baby chick hatches?**

mom comes back from geting food for baby. Dad goes to get food for him.

# Show What You Know!

Read each riddle. Draw a line from the riddle to the matching mom or dad.

I am an animal dad.
I do not have feathers.
I keep eggs safe in my belly.

I am an animal mom.
I do not have a pouch.
I teach my babies to fish.

We are an animal mom and dad.
We have long necks.
We take care of our baby together.

I am an animal mom.
I do not have wings.
I carry my baby in my pouch.

 Write one thing you learned from someone in your family.

_____

_____

# My Day at the Powwow

My name is Frederic Diaz. I am going to a powwow. A **powwow** is a Native American celebration. Come join in the fun!

## ❶ Make Cool Crafts

This lady shows people how to make a basket. She weaves baskets out of straw. Some Indian tribes make baskets. Others make flutes, jewelry, clay pots, and drums.

## ❷ Listen to Drums

This drum is loud! That's because several people play it at once. The drummers sing songs in Native American languages. My grandpa and uncles sing at powwows.

## ❸ Dance, Dance, Dance

This is me. I dance in the powwow dance. I move to the beat of the drums. I am a **grass dancer**.

In the old days, grass dancers were the first to dance at powwows. They would stomp the tall grass down so that others could dance. Now, people use lawn mowers! I sometimes win money for my dancing. Today, I came in second place.

### Three More Kinds of Powwow Dancers

fancy dancer

hoop dancer

jingle dancer

# Retell

Cut out the pictures. Use them to retell <u>My Day at the Powwow</u>.

# Learning Log

Draw pictures of three things you can see at a powwow. Write a sentence to tell about each picture.

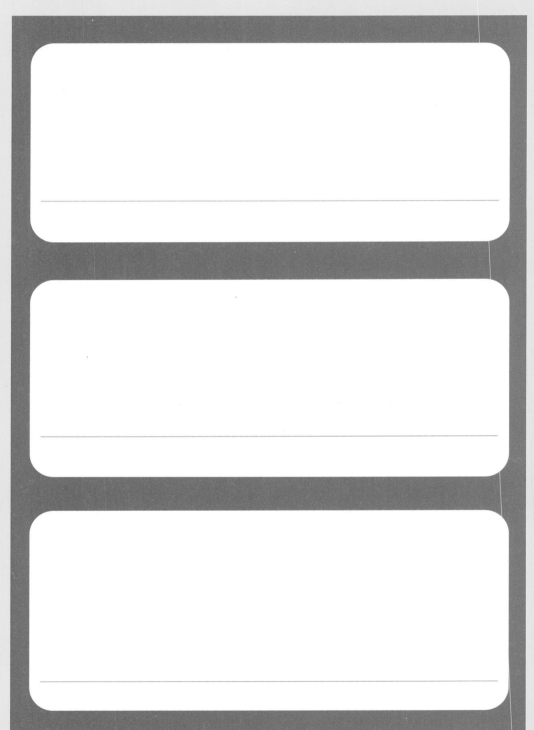

# Show What You Know!

Reread <u>What Native Americans Taught Us</u>.
Draw two things we have learned from Native Americans.
Write a sentence about each thing.

# 4

**Read Together**

# Amazing Plants!

Plants help people and animals in amazing ways.

### Birds Use Plants

Without plants, where would most birds live? This bird makes a home in a cactus. Many birds make **nests** on trees. Other animals, like raccoons, live in holes in trees.

gilded flicker

saguaro cactus

### We Eat Plants

Some plants taste good. They can be healthy, too. **Fruit** grows on plants. We make bread with a plant called **wheat**. Can you name other foods that come from plants?

watermelon

## We Use Plants to Make Things

Do you have clothes made from cotton? Cotton comes from cotton plants. We make many things from plant parts. We make **paper** out of chopped-up wood from trees. That means this book is made from a plant!

cotton

## Plants Make Air

How do we get air from plants? Plants make their own food from **sunlight** and water. When they do this, they let out something called oxygen (AHK-suh-jun). Oxygen is what we breathe.

## Plants Save the Land

Plants keep the land safe from wind and water. At the beach, wind blows the sand. Waves can wash it away. Beach grass helps. The **roots** of the grass hold the sand in place.

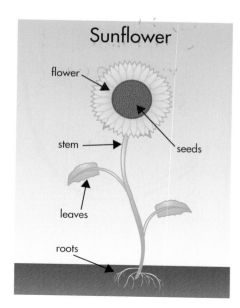

Sunflower

flower

stem

seeds

leaves

roots

# Retell

Cut out the pictures.
Use them to retell
<u>Amazing Plants!</u>

# Learning Log A+

In the middle of the flower, write what <u>Amazing Plants!</u> is mostly about. Hint: The introduction tells you. On each petal, write a fact from each part of the article.

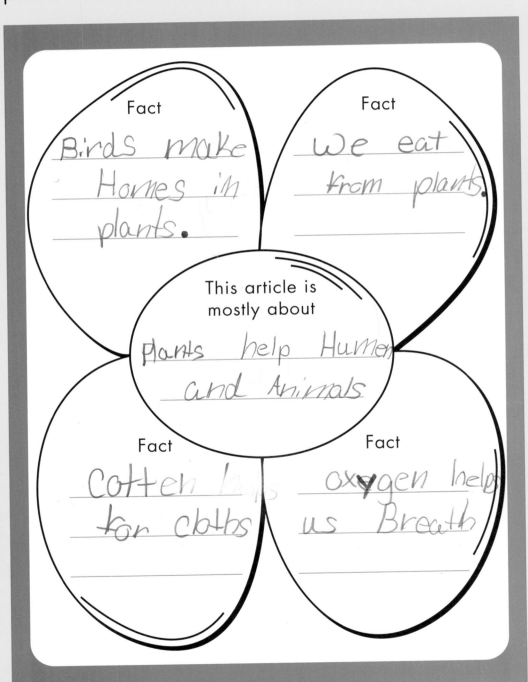

Fact

Birds make Homes in plants.

Fact

We eat from plants.

This article is mostly about

Plants help Human and Animals

Fact

Cotten is for cloths

Fact

oxygen help us Breath

# Show What You Know!

How does a pumpkin grow? Look at the pictures and figure out the steps. Write a number in each circle.

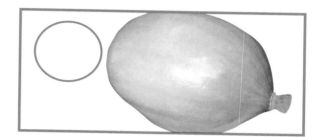

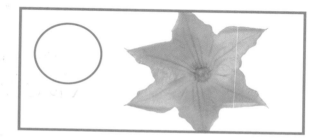

 What happens when the pumpkins are ripe?

_____

_____

_____

# 5

# Teeth Show What Animals Eat

Think about a meal you had this week. You might have had a hamburger. That's **meat**. You might have had an apple. That's a **plant**. Many people eat both plants and meat. So do many animals. Let's take a closer look inside these animals' mouths. The animal's teeth tell what it eats—plants, meat, or both.

## Meat Eater

Some animals eat only meat. Sharp, pointy teeth help animals tear into meat. This big cat uses its teeth to eat deer and birds.

leopard

## Plant Eater

Some animals eat only plants. Flat front teeth help animals bite into plants. This horse uses its teeth to eat hay, fruits, and vegetables.

horse

## Meat and Plant Eater

Some animals have both sharp teeth and flat teeth. That's because they eat meat and plants. This chimpanzee uses its sharp teeth to tear into meat, like wild pig. It uses its flat front teeth to bite into fruit.

chimpanzee

Look at the teeth of these animals. What kind of food do you think each eats?

crocodile

camel

baboon

# Retell

Cut out the pictures. Use them to retell <u>Teeth Show What Animals Eat</u>.

# Learning Log

Which animal fits under each heading? Draw a picture or write the name of the animal. Tell how that animal's teeth are special.

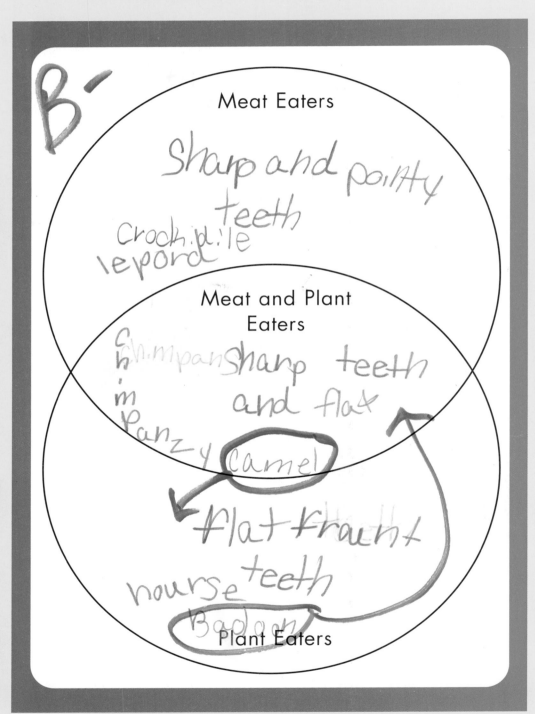

B-

**Meat Eaters**

Sharp and pointy teeth

Crockidile lepord

**Meat and Plant Eaters**

Chimpan Sharp teeth
im and flat
panzy Camel

flat fraicht teeth

nourse

Baboon

**Plant Eaters**

# Show What You Know!

Reread <u>Fun Dental Facts</u>.
Then, use the words in the box
to label the picture.

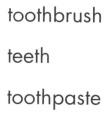

toothbrush

teeth

toothpaste

_____

_____

_____

Write two facts you learned about teeth.

Fact 1: _____

_____

Fact 2: _____

_____

# 6

# What Is a Fish?

How can you tell an animal is a fish?
Ask yourself four simple questions.

**① Does it live in water?**
All **fish** live in water. This
fish lives in the ocean. You
can also see fish in lakes,
rivers, and ponds.

**② Does it have fins?**
All fish have **fins**. Fish need
fins to move through the
water. A fish can have fins
on its back, belly, sides,
and tail. Fish fins are
different sizes, too.

fin

**③ Does it have gills?**
All fish have **gills**.
They use gills to
breathe. Water
goes through the
gills. Fish get air

The gills are in here.

from the water. What do you use to breathe?
You use your nose, mouth, and lungs.

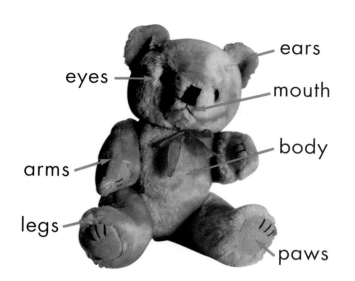

eyes — — ears

— mouth

arms — — body

legs — — paws

**❹ Stuff It**
A machine blows stuffing into the parts. Stuffing makes the parts plump. Then the parts are sewn to the bear's body.

**❺ Looking Good**
After the bear parts are put together, they get a good brushing. Now they are dressed and decorated.

**❻ Ready, Set, Go!**
The bears are packed into big boxes. Now they are ready to travel to their new homes and to make new friends.

# Learning Log

Fill in the chart below. Draw a picture for each step needed to make a teddy bear.

Step 1

Step 2

Step 3

Step 4

Step 5

Step 6

## ❹ Does it have a backbone?

All fish have a backbone. It is part of their **skeleton** (SKEL-uh-tin). Most of the time, you can't see a fish's skeleton. It is underneath the skin. This fish has clear skin, though.

backbone

## What is not a fish?

These animals live in water, but they are not fish! Here is why.

A jellyfish has no backbone. It is not a fish.

A crab moves with legs, not fins. It is not a fish.

A dolphin breathes through a blowhole, not through gills. It is not a fish.

Cut out the pictures.
Use them to retell
<u>What Is a Fish?</u>

# Learning Log

In each fish, write one thing that all fish have.

They have fins

They have Backbones

fish

They have gills

use gills to breath

 Write **fish** or **not fish** under each picture.

fish          fish          not fish

# Show What You Know!

Match the sentence with the correct picture.

I have four strong wings for
fast flying.

I have long, skinny legs for
running fast.

My song can be heard
very, very far away.

I can hold things that are
much heavier than I am.

 Write the fact that you think is the most amazing.

_____

_____

# 7

**Read Together**

# Winter Holidays

Winter holidays are a time for fun, family, and best of all, food. What holiday treats will you eat?

## Diwali

We eat **burfi** on Diwali. These soft sweets are made with nuts and spices. Some burfi are decorated with silver foil. Pretty!

## Ramadan

At the end of Ramadan, we have a feast. For our family's feast, we eat a spicy dish called **biryani** (beer-ee-AN-nee). It's made of rice, meat, and vegetables.

## Hanukkah

On Hanukkah, we eat crispy potato pancakes. They are called **latkes** (LAHT-kuz). We pour applesauce on top to make the pancakes even more delicious.

## Las Posadas

We eat candy on Las Posadas. The candy is hidden inside a **piñata** (peen-YAH-tuh). We hit the piñata with a stick until it breaks. Then, the candy spills out.

## Christmas

On Christmas, we eat **gingerbread**. We make gingerbread cookies and even a gingerbread house. The best part is decorating the house with icing and candy.

## Kwanzaa

In our home, on Kwanzaa, we eat an African fish dish called **ceebu jen** (CHE-boo JEN). It's yummy. We also eat American foods such as fried chicken and sweet-potato pie.

## Retell

Cut out the pictures.
Use them to retell
<u>Winter Holidays</u>.

# Learning Log

Tell how Christmas and Las Posadas are the same and different.

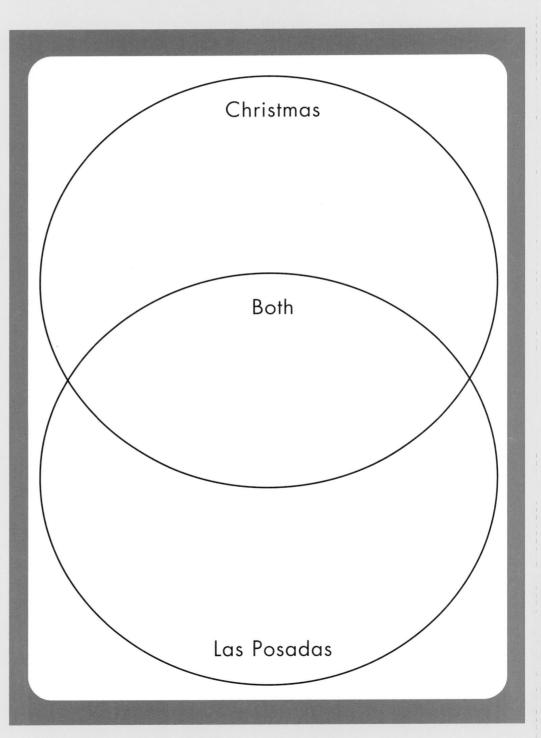

Christmas

Both

Las Posadas

# Show What You Know!

Reread <u>Flag Day</u>. Color the U.S. flag.

 Complete each sentence that tells about the flag.

1. The U.S. flag has _____ stars.

2. The U.S. flag has _____ stripes.

3. The colors of the U.S. flag are _____ ,

_____ , and _____ .

# 8

# Firefighters

Fires are very dangerous. Because of this, firefighters need special things to keep them safe. Firefighters wear special clothing called **turnout gear**. They use special tools to put out fires, too. Let's take a look.

**❶** A hard **helmet** covers the firefighter's head.

**❷** The **air pack** helps the firefighter breathe.

**❸** The **turnout coat** blocks out flames.

**❹** Tough **boots** keep the firefighter's feet safe.

**5** The firefighter uses a **fire tool** to break windows to let people out.

**6 Gloves** keep the firefighter's hands from getting burned.

**Fire-Safety Tip**
If your clothes catch fire, do this:

**STOP** where you are. Don't run.

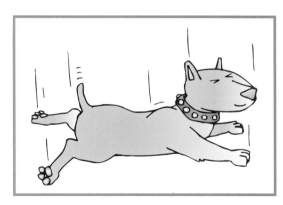

**DROP** to the ground.

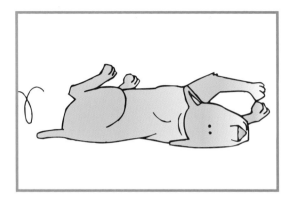

**ROLL** over and over. Cover your face with your hands.

# Retell

Cut out the pictures. Use them to retell the fire safety tips.

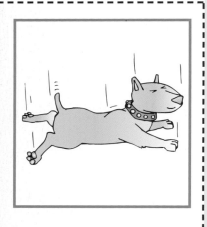

# Learning Log

Fill in the chart below. Draw or write what firefighters need to stay safe.

| Problem | Solution |
|---|---|
| Firefighters have a dangerous job. | Special clothes firefighters wear are _____. |
| | Special tools firefighters use are _____. |

# Show What You Know!

Reread <u>My Mom Is a Firefighter</u>.
Draw a picture of Victor's mom on the job.

 Write two sentences telling what she does.

_____

_____

# 9

# A Walk in the Rain Forest

What would it be like to walk in a tropical rain forest? You might see a **jaguar**! The jaguar hunts for food at night. It is a very good swimmer. It may follow an animal into the water during a chase! What else might you see?

Here's a colorful bird! It's a **toucan**. It has a large bill that is very sharp. The bill can break the fruits and berries that the toucan eats. As it eats, it drops seeds from the fruits and berries. New plants will grow from some of the seeds.

## Did you know . . .

Half of all the different kinds of plants and animals that live on Earth are found in rain forests!

Look! A butterfly rests on a tree. This kind of butterfly drinks juice from fruits. The fruits grow on the rain forest trees.

This tiny frog sits on a leaf. The frog is only as big as a person's thumbnail! Its bright colors warn other animals to stay away. It is not good to eat, because it is **poisonous**.

If you look carefully, you may see a **sloth** sleeping in a tree. A sloth is hard to see, because it is the same color as the tree trunk—grayish brown. Some sloths stay in the same tree for years! They hang and sleep upside down.

We are lucky to have so many rain forest plants and animals!

# Retell

Cut out the pictures. Use them to retell <u>A Walk in the Rain Forest</u>.

# Learning Log

Fill in the web. Write the name of a rain forest animal in each circle.

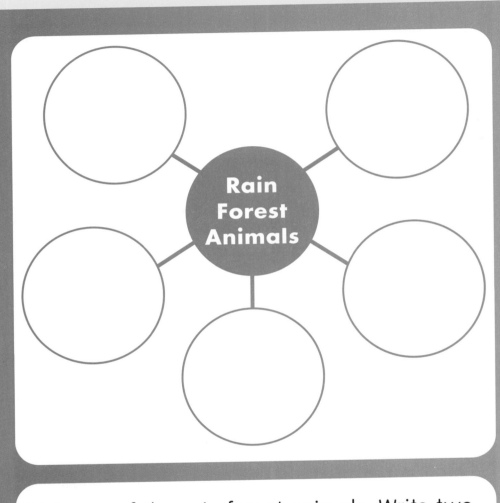

Rain Forest Animals

Pick one of the rain forest animals. Write two facts about it.

Fact 1: _____

Fact 2: _____

# Show What You Know!

Reread <u>Arctic Babies</u>. Then, fill in the chart below.

| Arctic Babies Keep Warm | |
| --- | --- |
| **Special Body** | **Mom Helps** |
| A seal pup has | |
| A musk ox baby has | |
| A polar bear cub has | |

What are some ways people keep warm in the cold? Write about one of them. Then draw a picture to show what you wrote about.

_____

_____

_____

_____

# 10

# Two Great

We remember George Washington and Abraham Lincoln in many ways.

**Washington's birthday is February 22.**

## George Washington

George Washington was our country's first president.

George Washington helped make our country free. Long ago, we were ruled by the **king** of England. George Washington led the fight to free us from England. That is why he is called "The Father of Our Country."

## Ways We Remember George Washington

The Washington Monument is in Washington, D.C.

Washington's face is on the one-dollar bill and the quarter.

# Presidents

Lincoln's birthday is February 12.

## Abraham Lincoln

Abraham Lincoln was our country's 16th President.

Abraham Lincoln helped end slavery in our country. Long ago, slaves were forced to work for other people. Many people knew this was wrong. Abraham Lincoln signed an order to end slavery.

## Ways We Remember Abraham Lincoln

The Lincoln Memorial is also in Washington, D.C.

Lincoln's face is on the five-dollar bill and the penny.

# Retell

Cut out the pictures.
Use them to retell
<u>Two Great Presidents</u>.

# Learning Log

Write things you know about each president.
Write ways they are the same in the center.

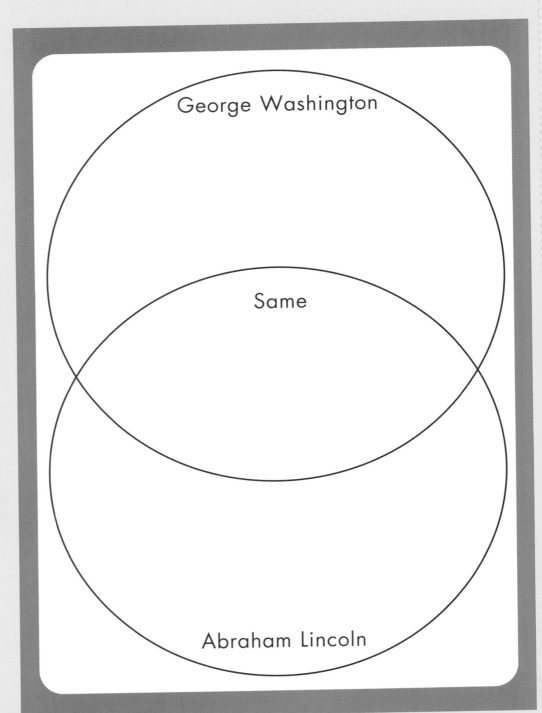

George Washington

Same

Abraham Lincoln

Back then, there were no cars or planes. To go far, people rode on horses or in a carriage.

Children loved to play, just like you do. They played with marbles and flew kites.

# Life Long Ago

What was life like when George Washington lived? There were no cameras then. So people today act out what life was like.

Back then, many children did not go to **school**. They learned how to read and write at home.

hat

bodice

apron

gown

petticoat

Back then, people did not wear the same **clothes** we wear today. Women wore dresses with big, long skirts.

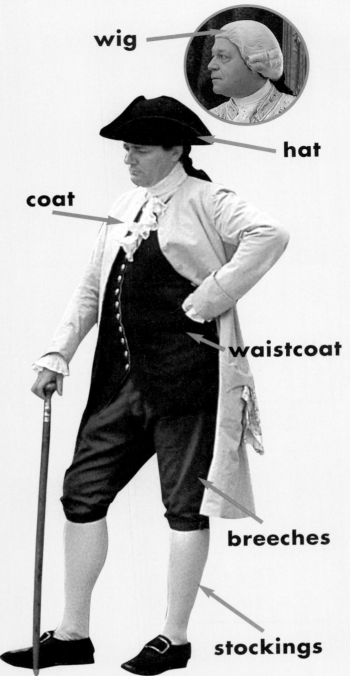

wig

hat

coat

waistcoat

breeches

stockings

Men wore stockings and short pants called **breeches** (BREE-chiz). Some people wore white wigs to look fancy.

# Show What You Know!

Draw a picture that shows something from George Washington's time and something today. Write some labels for your pictures.

| George Washington's Time | Today |
|---|---|
| clothing | |
| transportation | |
| games | |

What is something you like about life in George Washington's time?

_____

_____

# Let It Rain or Snow

Is it rainy where you live today? If so, what caused it to rain? Rain and snow are formed inside a cloud. Here's how.

### Clouds Bring Rain

Clouds are made of tiny drops of water. As the drops of water come together, they make bigger drops. These big drops of water are heavy enough to fall to the earth as rain.

### Clouds Bring Snow

When the tiny drops of water in a cloud get very cold, the drops of water turn to ice crystals. Snowflakes are made when the tiny ice crystals stick together.

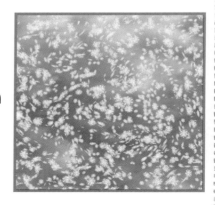

## Different Clouds Bring

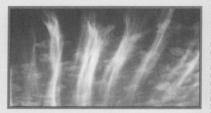

**Cumulus clouds** are white and puffy. You see them in sunny skies.

**Cirrus clouds** are thin and look like feathers. They often mean that rain is coming.

## Weather Map

Seattle
Helena
Bismarck
Minneapolis
Boston
New York
Salt Lake City
Chicago
Washington, D.C.
Denver
Los Angeles
Phoenix
Memphis
Atlanta
Dallas
New Orleans
Miami

**Map Key**

Rain

### Helful Rain

Rain gives plants water to drink. First, rain sinks into the ground. Then, plants suck up the rainwater through their roots.

### Harmful Rain

Rain can also cause a flood. Many floods happen when rain makes a river or lake too full. Other floods happen when too much rain falls too fast. The water spills into homes and fills up streets.

# Different Weather

**Stratus clouds** are a sheet of low, gray clouds. They often bring light rain or snow.

**Cumulonimbus clouds** are dark and piled up high. They often bring thunderstorms.

# Retell

Cut out the pictures.
Use them to retell
<u>Let It Rain or Snow</u>.

# Learning Log

Fill in the chart below. Then write the good and bad effects of rain.

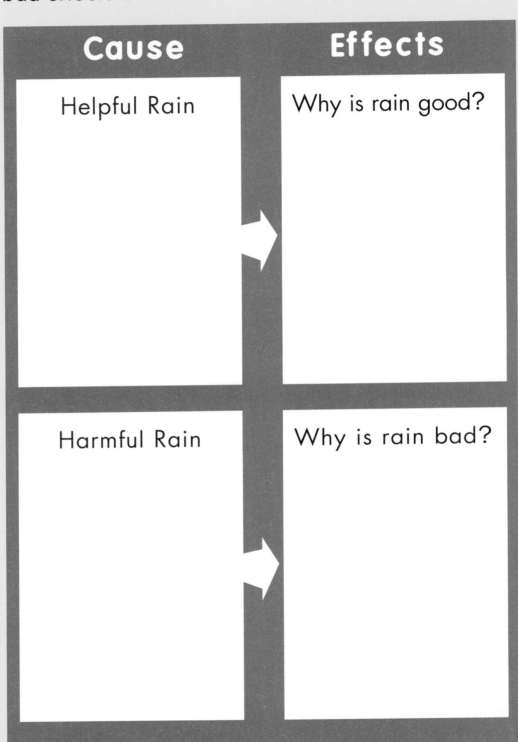

| Cause | Effects |
|---|---|
| Helpful Rain | Why is rain good? |
| Harmful Rain | Why is rain bad? |

# Show What You Know!

Reread <u>Wind and Sun</u>. Then, look at each picture.

Circle  if the picture shows helpful weather.

Circle  if the picture shows harmful weather.

# 12

# Let's Take a Trip to the Solar System

### The Sun

Put on your sunglasses! Our first stop is the bright sun. The sun is a giant star. All nine planets **orbit**, or move in circles around, the sun.

### Mercury

You are visiting the planet closest to the sun. Mercury has **craters**, or holes, on its surface. Watch your step!

### Venus

Next is Venus, the hottest planet in the solar system. Its hot, yellow gas clouds are **poison**.

### Earth

Welcome home! Our planet has water, land, and white clouds. Earth is the only planet we know that has living things.

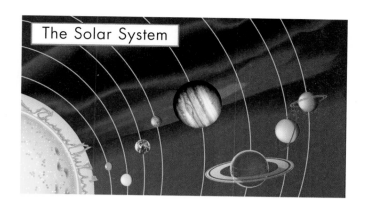

The Solar System

## Mars

This is Earth's neighbor. Mars is called the Red Planet. Scientists have sent robots to study Mars.

## Jupiter

Look at this big planet made of gas. Do you see Jupiter's Great Red Spot? It's a **hurricane** that has been blowing for at least 300 years.

## Saturn

Next is another planet made of gas. Saturn has about 1,000 rings made of dust and ice.

## Uranus and Neptune

Turn on the heat! Uranus and Neptune are cold gas planets. Wind swirls fast on Neptune!

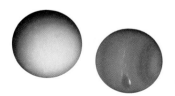

ARE YOU READY TO GO HOME?

# Retell

Cut out the pictures. Use them to retell <u>Let's Take a Trip to the Solar System</u>.

# Learning Log

Fill in the chart. Draw a picture of the planet. Write one fact you learned.

| Planet | What It Looks Like | One Fact I Learned |
|---|---|---|
| Venus | | |
| Earth | | |
| Mars | | |
| Jupiter | | |

# Show What You Know!

Reread <u>Astronaut</u>. Draw a picture of an astronaut working in space.

WRITE  Write two facts you learned.

Fact 1: _____

_____

Fact 2: _____

_____

# 13

# Animals Helping

People sometimes face special **problems**. They may need help getting from place to place. Or they may need help if they can't use their hands or arms. Animals can help **solve** these problems. Let's see how animals help people.

Glimmer is training to be a **guide dog** for the blind. Eamon, age 5, teaches her to wait for her food. Guide dogs can't stop and eat anytime they want. They must pay attention to keep their owners safe.

Eamon and his family train Glimmer and other guide dogs.

Dogs aren't the only animals that can help the blind. Twinkie is a miniature, or little, **horse**. Mini horses are very smart, calm, and quiet. After Twinkie is trained, she works as a guide horse for the blind.

Twinkie wears sneakers to protect her feet.

# People

Dolphins can help people. It's hard for some people to move easily. **Exercise**, like swimming, helps them move better. People like to swim with dolphins. Dolphins can give kisses when the people do a good job!

Dolphins are very friendly.

Monkeys help people who cannot move their arms or hands. How? These little monkeys have hands that are like people's hands. So they can do things like turn lights on and off and take the tops

Capuchin monkey

off jars. They can even put a CD or video in a player and start it! Plus the monkeys are very friendly. Their owners love having them around.

# Retell

Cut out the pictures. Use them to retell <u>Animals Helping People</u>.

# Learning Log

Read about each person. Then tell how an animal helps the person.

| Problem | Solution |
|---|---|
| A blind person may need help going places. | |
| A person who can't move easily may need exercise. | |
| A person who can't move his arms or hands may need help to do things at home. | |

# Show What You Know!

Draw some of the things that we make or eat from what animals give us. Label each thing.

| | |
|---|---|
| What We Make to Wear | What We Make to Eat |

 Write a thank-you note to an animal you read about.

Dear _____ ,

_____

_____

_____

_____

Your friend,

_____

# 14

**Read Together**

# We Recycle!

People throw away a lot of trash. This **causes** a lot of waste. We're running out of places to put it all. That's why we recycle. What happens to trash that is recycled?

## Old Trash

What happens to old **cans**? They are heated until they melt. As they cool, they harden. They are shaped into something new!

Old **newspaper** is chopped up and mixed with water. Then it goes into a big dryer. It comes out as fluff. Now it can be used as something new!

**Plastic bottles** are washed. Then, they are melted. As the plastic cools, it is spun into thread. The thread will be used for something new!

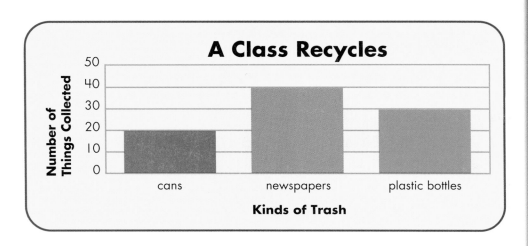

**A Class Recycles**

Number of Things Collected

50
40
30
20
10
0

cans | newspapers | plastic bottles

**Kinds of Trash**

# Something New

The cans are used to make a **bicycle**. The frame of this bicycle is made from 125 cans.

The paper fluff is sold in pet stores. It makes great **bedding** for small animals. The paper keeps this hamster warm and dry.

A machine weaves the thread into **cloth** called fleece. It takes 25 bottles to make a fleece coat. The coat is very soft. It doesn't feel like plastic at all!

# Retell

Cut out the pictures. Use them to retell <u>We Recycle!</u>

✂

# Learning Log

Fill in the chart below. Draw or write what happens when you recycle things.

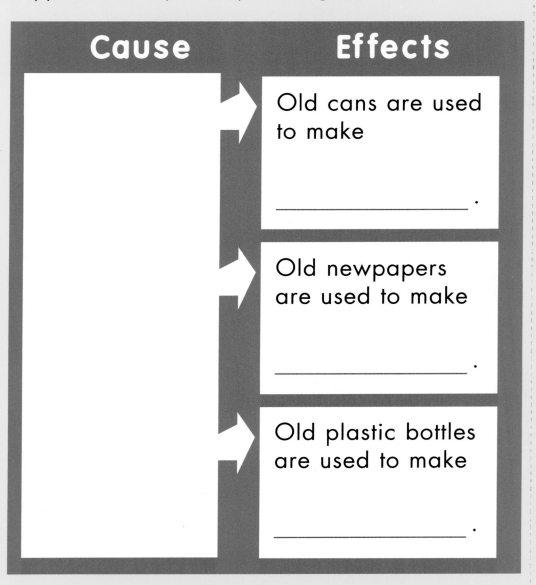

| Cause | Effects |
|---|---|
| | Old cans are used to make _____. |
| | Old newpapers are used to make _____. |
| | Old plastic bottles are used to make _____. |

Draw one thing you use that was recycled.

# Show What You Know!

Circle the things that help Earth.
Put an **X** on the things that do not help.

 Write what you do to reduce, reuse, and recycle.

I reduce _____.

I reuse _____.

I recycle _____.

# 15

# Africa

Africa is a big continent. A **continent** is a very large piece of land. There are seven continents on Earth.

The biggest desert on Earth is in Africa. This desert is called the Sahara Desert. It is almost as big as the United States! Here are some interesting things in Africa.

## Giraffe

This baby giraffe has a long way to grow. One day it will be as tall as its mom. Then it will reach the tops of the trees.

## Pitcher Plant

Bugs watch out! This plant looks yummy. But, it will eat the bugs who stop for a snack.

## Painted Walls

What can you make with mud? These walls were built with dried mud. Then they were painted with beautiful colors.

# Africa

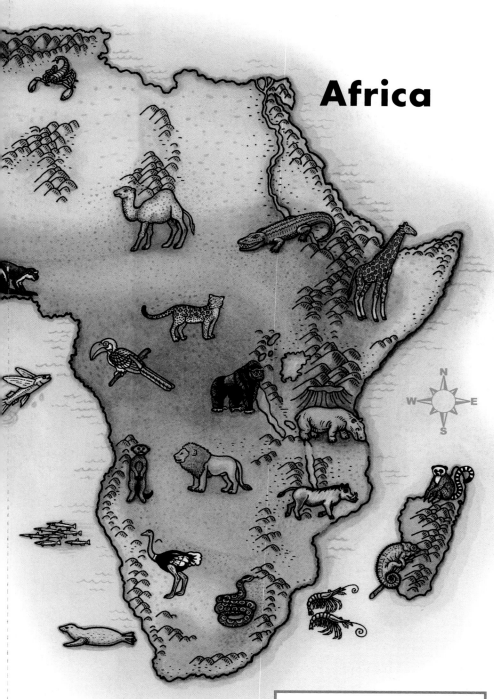

## Map Key

 Mountain

Desert

Savanna

Dry Woodland

Rain Forest

# Retell

Cut out the pictures. Use them to retell Africa.

# Learning Log

Fill in the chart below. Compare Africa to your hometown.

| Africa | My Hometown |
| --- | --- |
| Animal in Africa | Animal Where I Live |
| Tree or Plant in Africa | Tree or Plant Where I Live |
| House in Africa | House Where I Live |

# Show What You Know!

Reread <u>Asia</u>. Then, match the sentence to the correct picture.

I am the tallest
mountain on Earth.

(orangutan)

I live in trees in
the rain forest.

(reindeer)

I run fast across
the snow.

(Mount Everest)

 Write how Asia is different from where you live.

_____

_____

_____

_____

# Credits

**Text:** "Amazing Nests," "How Are Teddy Bears Made?," "From Apples to Applesauce," "Animal Moms and Dads," "My Day at the Powwow," "What Native Americans Taught Us," "Amazing Plants," "In the Pumpkin Patch," "Teeth Show What Animals Eat," "Fun Dental Facts," "What Is a Fish?," "Insect Olympics," "Winter Holidays," "Flag Day," "Firefighters," "My Mom Is a Firefighter," "A Walk in the Rain Forest," "Arctic Babies," "Two Great Presidents," "Life Long Ago," "Let It Rain or Snow," "Wind and Sun," "Let's Take a Trip to the Solar System," "Astronaut," "Animals Helping," "From Farm to You," "We Recycle," "We Help the Earth," "Africa," and "Asia" are reprinted from SCHOLASTIC NEWS. Copyright © 1995, 1996, 1998, 1999, 2000, 2001, 2002, 2003, 2004, 2005 by Scholastic Inc. Reprinted by permission.

**Images:** Cover: Native American © Suzanne Murphy/Getty Images; Sunflower © Royalty-Free/Corbis; Penguins © Frank Krahmer/Zefa/Corbis; Saturn © Jonathan Fox/Brand X Pictures/Jupiter Images. Page 4: (left) John Cancalosi/DRK Photo; (right) Ron Austing/Frank K. Lane Picture Library/Corbis; (bottom left) Rita Lascaro; (bottom right) Jason Robinson. Page 5: (illustration, top) Karen Sevaly; (illustration, bottom) Jason Robinson. Page 6: Adam Riesner, (middle) Andrew Francke, all images courtesy of the Vermont Teddy Bear Factory. Page 7: (from top) Copyright © 2007 Scholastic and its licensors. All rights reserved; Adam Riesner, all images courtesy of the Vermont Teddy Bear Factory. Page 8: (illustration) Brian LaRossa. Pages 9–10: (photos) Larry Kinneman/Ziegler Studio/Knaus Foods Applesauce. Page 10: (illustration) Brian LaRossa. Page 12: (top) Fritz Poelking/Alamy; (bottom) Bruno P. Zehnder/Alamy. Page 13: (top) Doug Allan/Animals Animals; (bottom) Frans Lanting/Minden; (map) Mapman/Scholastic. Page 14: (left) Hans Reinhard/Zefa/Corbis; (middle) Bryan & Cherry Alexander/Arctic Photo. Page 15: (top) Sanford Agliolo/Corbis; (bottom) Rudie Kuiter/SeaPics.com. Page 16: (top) Fritz Prenzel/Animals Animals; (bottom) M. Philip Kahl Jr./Photo Researchers. Page 17: Brian LaRossa. Page 18: (from top) Mary Pierpont; Spencer Grant/PhotoEdit; Robert W. Madden, National Geographic Image Collection. Page 19: (top) Mary Pierpont; (left) Lindsay Hebberd; (middle) Cleve Bryant/PhotoEdit; (right) Michael Newman/PhotoEdit. Page 21: Eastcott-Momatiuk/Woodfin Camp. Page 22: (top) Wolfgang Kaehler/Liaison International; (bottom) M. Greenlar/The Image Works. Page 24: (left) Tom Vezo/Peter Arnold; (right) David Frazier/The Image Works; (bottom) Anthony Nex/Corbis. Page 25: (from top) Camara Lucida/Stock Photo; Richard Hamilton Smith/Corbis; Grant Faint/Getty Images; (illustration) Brian LaRossa. Page 26: (illustration) Holly Grundon. Page 27: (top) Myrleen Ferguson Cate/PhotoEdit; (middle) Josef Scalea/Corbis; (bottom left) Sandy Mayer; (bottom center) David Young-Wolff/PhotoEdit; (bottom right) Larry Lefever/Grant Heilman. Page 28: (top) Jim Strawser/Grant Heilman; (middle left) Steven Diamond; (middle center) R.J. Erwin/Photo Researchers; (middle right) Sandy Mayer; (bottom) Josef Scalea/Corbis. Page 30: (top) David A. Northcott/Corbis; (bottom) Sylvain Cordier/Photo Researchers. Page 31: (top) Manoj Shah/Tony Stone; (middle) Bob Walden/Australian Library/Corbis. Page 33: (top) SODA; (bottom) James Levin/Studio 10. Page 34: (bottom) Dave J. Anthony/Getty Images. Page 35: Kelly Kennedy. Page 36: (top) Tobias Bernhard/OSF; (middle) Michael P. Gadomski/Photo Researchers. Page 37: (from top) Jeff Rotman; Mark Conlin/Getty Images; Masa Ushioda/SeaPics.com; M.C. Chamberlain/DRK Photo. Page 38: (illustration, top) Jane Yamada; (illustrations, bottom) Ivy Rutzky. Page 39: (photos from top) Hyungwon Kang/Reuters/Corbis; Naturfoto Honal/Corbis; (illustrations) Kelly Kennedy. Page 40: (photos from top) Wolfgang Kaehler/Corbis; Tom Young/Corbis; (illustrations, top & bottom left) Kelly Kennedy; (illustration, bottom right) Ivy Rutzky. Page 42: (from top) James Levin/Studio 10; Michael Newman/PhotoEdit; Ted Spiegel/Corbis. Page 43: (from top) Robert Frerck/Corbis; Ariel Skelley/Corbis; Susan Kuklin/Photo Researchers. Page 45: (top) Photolink/Corbis; (bottom) Ron Brown/SuperStock. Page 46: (top left) Owen Franken/Corbis; (top right) The Granger Collection, New York; (center) New York Public Library Picture Collection; (bottom) NASA. Page 48: Courtesy of Securitex. Page 49: Brian LaRossa. Page 51: Tim McKinney. Page 52: (top) Tim McKinney; (bottom) Bill Stormont/Corbis. Page 54: (top) John Giustina/Giust/Bruce Coleman Inc.; (bottom) Kevin Schafer/Corbis. Page 55: (map) Mapman/Scholastic; (photos, from top) Fabio Colobini/Animals Animals; James P. Rowan/DRK Photo; Staffen Widstrand/Corbis. Page 57: Kevin Schafer/Getty Images. Page 58: (top) Dominique Braud/Dembinsky; (bottom) T. Davis/W. Bilenduke/Getty Images. Page 60: (top) The Granger Collection, NY; (bottom left) Hisham F. Ibrahim/Getty Images. Page 61: (top) The Granger Collection, NY; (bottom left) Photolink/Getty Images. Page 63: (left, top & bottom) Colonial Williamsburg Foundation, Williamsburg, VA; (right) Photographs by Russ Kendall from *Mary Geddy's Day* by Kate Waters. Photographs copyright © 1999 by Russ Kendall. Reprinted by permission of Scholastic. Page 64: (left & top right) Colonial Williamsburg Foundation, Williamsburg, VA; (bottom right) Photographs by Russ Kendall from *Mary Geddy's Day* by Kate Waters. Photographs copyright © 1999 by Russ Kendall. Reprinted by permission of Scholastic. Page 66: (top) Craig Tuttle/Corbis; (middle) Matthias Kulka/Corbis; (bottom left) Don & Pat Valenti/Tony Stone; (bottom right) IFA/Peter Arnold. Page 67: (map) Brian LaRossa; (photos, from top) Roy Morsch/Corbis; (middle) AFP Corbis; (bottom left) Kent Wood/Photo Researchers; (bottom right) Dr. Dan Sudia/Photo Researchers. Page 69: (top) Tom Mareschal/Getty Images; (bottom) Mike Schroder/Peter Arnold. Page 70: (top) Jim Zuckerman/Corbis; (bottom) Royalty-Free/Corbis. Page 71: Kelly Kennedy. Page 72: (from top) NASA; Antonio M. Rosario/Getty Images; (2) NASA. Page 73: (illustration) Ian Worpole; (top) NASA. Pages 75–76: NASA. Page 78: (top) Cindy Miller; (bottom) Lisa Carpenter. Page 79: (top) Tom Kane/Black Star; (bottom) Jim Bourg/Reuters/Corbis. Page 81: (top) Grant Heilman/Grant Heilman Photography; (bottom) SuperStock. Page 82: (photo) Larry Lefever/Grant Heilman; (illustrations) Ellen Appleby. Page 84: (from top) Fogstock/Alamy; Royalty-Free/Corbis; Ron Chapple/Alamy. Page 85: (from top) Peter Griffith/Masterfile; Robert Pickett/Corbis; Gail Mooney. Page 87: (top) Michael H. Francis; (bottom left) PictureQuest; (bottom right) Mike Severns/Tony Stone. Page 88: (top left) David Young-Wolff/PhotoEdit; (top right) Michael H. Francis; (bottom left) PictureQuest; (bottom right) John Cancalosi/DRK Photo. Page 89: Kelly Kennedy. Page 90: (map) Anne Stanley; (photo, top) Corbis; (2) SuperStock. Page 93: (map) Anne Stanley; (photo) Frans Lanting/Corbis. Page 94: (top) Nicholas DeVore/Tony Stone; (bottom) Bryan & Cherry Alexander/Arctic Photos.

Editor: Mela Ottaiano
Cover Design: Jorge J. Namerow